Reckless

Reckless

Lesley Choyce

Orca currents

ORCA BOOK PUBLISHERS

Library and Archives Canada Cataloguing in Publication

Choyce, Lesley, 1951-
Reckless / written by Lesley Choyce.
(Orca currents)

Issued in print and electronic formats.
ISBN 978-1-55469-223-1 (pbk.).—ISBN 978-1-55469-225-5 (pdf).—
ISBN 978-1-55469-525-6 (epub)

I. Title. II. Series: Orca currents
PS8555.H668R425 2010   jc813'.54   C2009-906833-8

First published in the United States, 2010
Library of Congress Control Number: 2009940766

Summary: While riding his dirt bike on an abandoned logging road,
Josh encounters a Vietnam veteran who has been living in the wilderness
for forty years, and the two develop an unusual friendship.

MIX
Paper from
responsible sources
FSC® C016245
www.fsc.org

*Orca Book Publishers is dedicated to preserving the environment and has
printed this book on Forest Stewardship Council® certified paper.*

Orca Book Publishers gratefully acknowledges the support for its
publishing programs provided by the following agencies: the Government
of Canada through the Canada Book Fund and the Canada Council for the Arts,
and the Province of British Columbia through the BC Arts Council
and the Book Publishing Tax Credit.

Cover photograph by Getty Images
Author photo by Nancy Snow

ORCA BOOK PUBLISHERS
www.orcabook.com

Printed and bound in Canada.

20 19 18 17 • 6 5 4 3

Chapter One

I was having a bad day. I woke up a half hour late and missed my bus. I had to walk to school. This made me late for my English test, so I didn't have time to finish it. It's safe to say I failed it. What is it with poetry anyway?

I had no lunch and no lunch money, and I couldn't bring myself to beg from anyone in school. Sonia, *the* Sonia, who had said I was cute and that she wanted to go out with me, changed her mind. I could tell because she was talking to Anton when I walked by her. She totally ignored me.

On the way to the bus in the afternoon, I stepped in a fresh pile of dog crap. This made me less than popular on the bus, so I got out halfway and walked the rest of the way home.

At home, I threw my shoes in the garbage can outside and went in to put on my old hiking boots and biking clothes. Without saying hello to my mom, who was upstairs, I grabbed my helmet and headed for the shed. I was almost out the door when I remembered. Leave a note.

Home from school. Gone to the woods. Be back by dark.

Josh

We'd had many arguments about the dirt bike. This was our compromise.

I grabbed the cell phone from the top of the fridge—another compromise—and stuffed it into my pocket.

My old four-stroke Kawasaki dirt bike looked as ragged and beat-up as ever. But it was my only friend right then. Its smell of leaking oil made me smile. I kicked the stand and walked it into the yard, poured gas into the tank and then cranked it over. As it roared to life, the neighbor's dog started barking. I knew my mom would hear it and want to come out to talk to me. I didn't want to talk. I popped on the helmet, jumped on the beast, hit the clutch and put it in first gear. I gave her some gas, and we were off.

One good thing about living in a little town in the middle of nowhere is that you are surrounded by a lot of empty space. Well, not empty really. But there is a lot of land with no people. Hopevale was on the edge of a huge government-owned forest. There were logging roads left over from the old days, and one connected with the road I lived on. It was only a two-minute roar—and I do mean roar—to where I could leave civilization behind. And that's what I did.

I downshifted, took the turn a bit too fast and dipped into the ditch that was intended to keep out SUVs, ATVs and bikers off the logging road. I lifted off the seat and revved hard on the gas as my knobby tires clawed at the gravel. I shot out of the ditch and over the embankment, taking a few inches of air. The forest looked dark and inviting. I leveled out and cranked my bike wide-open for the first straight stretch.

I wanted to get deep into the forest as quickly as I could.

The logging road was rutted and full of rocks. Tree branches hung down over the trail. Sometimes the wind knocked maple limbs down onto the path. Once I found an entire tree blocking the trail. I was riding recklessly the day I found that tree. I forgot that the trail was always changing. I have a dent over the gas tank and a scar on my left knee from that day.

But we learn from our mistakes, right?

I tend to learn the hard way.

I learned to double-clutch so I could shift from second to fourth without stalling or losing speed. I didn't have third gear. I learned to keep my weight off the seat, feet on the pegs, when riding over a rough road. And roads don't get much rougher than this weathered, potholed, rock-strewn trail. I had learned how to control the rear end of the bike as it fishtailed through the sand and gravel on the trail.

The bike and the trail taught me all I needed to know. But I wasn't prepared for what happened next.

As I raced deep into the woods, I put my day behind me. What did I care about poetry or Sonia or dog crap? None of that mattered now.

I loved the throaty roar of the old engine. Yet, once I'd gone a half hour or so into the forest and scared away every living creature, I'd usually cut the engine. I'd let the ringing in my ears fade and sit in the quiet of the woods. I loved that as much as I liked the buzz of riding. I guess that makes me a bit weird.

I wanted to get as far from Hopevale as fast as I could. There was no one else on the trail. I whizzed through the shallow stream that crosses with the trail without getting wet. I popped a wheelie on a smooth stretch. I ducked under a couple of poplars bending over the trail. I spun gravel, bounced over rocks and rode through dry leaves that swirled around me like a tornado.

Just before Loggerman Creek the trail makes a ninety-degree turn to the north. The turn is sand and gravel. It's perfect for cranking hard, leaning low to the right, dragging my boot and letting the back wheel slide. I've fallen here before, but I usually nailed it.

This time was different. I went low and felt the rear wheel slide. While my right foot skimmed along the ground, I gave her a full throttle and shot out of the turn. I was concentrating so much on the turn that I didn't look where I was going.

When I was upright again, a shaft of sunlight pierced through the trees, blinding me. But I knew this trail, so I kept giving her gas.

That's when I saw him.

A crazy old man with a beard stood in the middle of the logging road. He looked straight at me with fierce blue eyes.

I jammed hard to the right again and hit the brakes. I had no choice but to drop the bike. I stayed with it though, and I thought I might miss him.

But I didn't.

I was sliding with the bike over painful gravel when I slammed into him. Hard. He toppled over me as the bike dragged me into a big rock.

I felt pain shoot through my right leg and up my side. The engine had stalled. I tore off my glove and I reached out. I accidentally touched the hot exhaust pipe and screamed from the pain. My side hurt more as I dragged myself out from under the bike. I tried to stand and fell into the bushes at the side of the trail. I staggered to my feet, tore off my helmet and looked down at the crumpled figure on the road. He wasn't moving.

I was sure I had killed him. The blood drained out of my head. I was afraid to approach him. I needed to get help. I took several deep breaths and found myself shaking. Hold it together, I told myself. Just hold it together.

I looked down and saw raw skin and blood where my jeans had been torn. I touched my ribs and felt the pain there too. But I was pretty sure nothing was broken. But him. How was I going to help this crazy old man?

I pulled out my cell phone and was thrilled to see that it still worked. But there was no signal. I knew that it didn't work deep in the forest. I had never told my parents that.

I had to see if he was still alive. I stumbled forward and said in a shaky voice, "Yo. Are you okay? I'm sorry, man. It wasn't my fault."

There was no answer. He was lying there curled up, facing away from me. I tried to remember first aid. What was I supposed to do? Not move him? Check to see if he is breathing?

Cautiously, I bent over. I tried to listen for breath, but my own breathing was so ragged and my heart was pumping in my ears so loudly I couldn't hear anything. I kneeled beside him and noticed the smell. This guy hadn't had a bath in a long, long time. A Boston Red Sox baseball cap, frayed and grimy, was on the ground beside him.

That's when it clicked. This guy was the hermit of Loggerman Creek. The hermit had been living out here since before I was born.

And now I had killed him.

I got the courage to touch his shoulder. "Hey," I yelled. "Please!"

Please what? Please be alive, I guess. Please don't let this happen.

"I'm sorry," I said. He still didn't move.

I moved around to check out the crumpled old man. His face looked ancient with deep creases. His beard was gray and brown. I wondered if the police would put me in jail. This could not be happening.

I was still staring at his face when suddenly the eyes opened. Those fierce eyes of a madman. I let out a scream.

He stared up at me. He let out a moan that sounded inhuman.

Then he pushed himself up, his eyes still locked on mine.

I shuffled backward as he tried to stand. He coughed several times, spit blood onto the ground. He looked wild and angry. I wanted to say I was sorry again, but I had lost my ability to speak. I was happy he was alive, but now this guy looked capable of murder.

He faltered as he finally made it to his feet. Then he bent over to pick up the ball cap. He slapped it on his leg and then put it on his head. "You have no right," he shouted at me. "You have no right to be out here with that infernal noise machine!" He turned and glared at the bike.

"It was an accident," I whispered, hoping I could calm him.

"Spewing smoke, scaring the deer, the birds. Digging and gouging the earth. Why do you come here?" He looked like he was about to hit me.

"You need to be taught a lesson." He spat more blood.

I thought he was going to come at me—he was standing with both fists raised—but he turned and looked at my bike. The front wheel was bent badly and so was the fork. The gas tank had new dents. It looked more pathetic than ever. He seemed to forget about me and hobbled toward my bike. He lifted it upright and then looked back at me. "Enough," he said.

Then he began walking the bike into the forest. With the bent front fork and rim, it was not easy for him to roll it forward.

It dawned on me that he was stealing my bike. "Hey!" I yelled, taking a few steps toward him. "That's mine."

He stopped and looked back. That crazy look again. "Hey," he said, mimicking me. "It's not always about you. Learn that one." And he rolled my bike away again.

I took a few steps toward him, but I stopped. Who knew what he might do? But it was my bike. That's when I said, "I guess it is true. I guess they are right. You are crazy."

The hermit stopped again and turned. "Get out. Go home. Leave me alone."

I watched until he was swallowed by the forest. I felt the pain in my side more than ever now.

I picked up my helmet and started the long painful walk home. The forest didn't seem so friendly anymore.

Chapter Two

I couldn't believe how long it took me to walk home. About halfway I discovered I had cell phone reception. I considered calling home for help. But I knew I'd be in big trouble.

Once it started to get dark, I was spooked. I heard noises around me in the trees. There were bears out here,

I knew, and a few coyotes. And what if that old crazy man decided to come after me? I felt a shiver go through me.

After getting slapped in the face a couple of times with branches, I slowed my pace. I felt like sitting down to get my heart to stop racing and regain my cool, but I knew I better trudge on. I decided to call my friend, Kyle. I had to hear a human voice. The word *friend* might have been an exaggeration. Kyle didn't really have any friends. He kept so much to himself that no one knew much about him. But he seemed to know everything there was to know on any subject, local or international. I figured he'd read all the encyclopedias on the Internet.

I phoned his cell, and he answered the first ring.

"Kyle, it's me, Josh," I said.

"Josh, where are you at?" he asked. "I can hardly hear you."

The connection was really bad. "I'm in the woods, walking home. I, uh, had some trouble with the bike."

"It's getting pretty dark. Are you okay? What happened?"

I told him my story. It helped to have someone to talk to.

"You plowed into the hermit of Loggerman Creek?" he asked.

"Yeah, I guess I did. He scared the crap out of me."

"You're lucky he didn't kill you, dude."

"Why?" I asked.

"I think I better tell you later."

"Okay. Listen, I better save my battery. I'll call you later. If I don't call though…" I swallowed hard and couldn't finish.

"If you don't call me by eight, I'll get help. You're on the old logging road, right?"

"Yep."

"You want me to get a flashlight and meet up with you?"

"No," I said. "But thanks."

My parents were eating dinner when I arrived. They started yelling at me, asking where I'd been. I quickly walked on through the house and mumbled something in response. I ran upstairs to my room, ripped off my clothes and took a shower. I gave Kyle a quick call to say I was safe. Then I walked downstairs as if nothing had happened.

"Where were you?" my mom demanded.

"I was just hanging out with Kyle," I lied. "Sorry about the time. Guess I lost track."

They knew I was lying. They knew I'd been out in the woods on the bike, but they didn't push it.

My mom noticed the scratches on my face. "You okay?"

"Yeah, I'm fine."

They looked more than a little ticked off. After a long minute or two of silence, I added, "Sorry." That was often enough to get me off the hook. They probably wouldn't notice the bike was gone. The shed was pretty much my territory. My father hardly ever went there.

Back in my room, I started getting angry about losing my bike. Hitting the old guy was an accident. He shouldn't have taken my bike. No dirt bike meant no life as far as I was concerned. All I had to do was call the police, right? My bike was stolen, and I knew who had it.

If I got the cops involved, though, it would get messy. My parents would never let me go into the woods again. I lay on my bed, and I couldn't get the image of that guy's angry face out of my head. I had heard of the hermit of Loggerman Creek but never paid much attention to the stories. I phoned Kyle. He would have the scoop.

"He's been out there living alone for over forty years," Kyle said. "That's what I've been told. He'd been a soldier in the Vietnam War. They say he killed one hundred men. He kept count. On the day he killed his one-hundredth enemy soldier, he cracked. He deserted and ran. Eventually he came back here, went into the woods and pretty well never came out."

"Why would he do that?" I asked.

"He thinks he can still be arrested," said Kyle. "A couple of older guys who go in there on ATVs have tried to tell him that an amnesty was declared a long time back. No one is going to put him in prison. But he doesn't believe them. The forest rangers say he runs and hides whenever they go near his shack.

He's scared to death of anyone in a uniform. I bet he'd try to kill anyone who tried to make him leave the woods."

"How does he live?" I asked.

"He fishes, I think. Grows some of his own food. Kills a few rabbits. Dave Jenkins and some other ATV guys take him some supplies once in a while," Kyle said. "He tells them crazy stories about trees talking to him and UFOS. And helicopters. He hates helicopters more than anything. Something to do with Vietnam."

"You ever meet him?" I asked.

"No way. I never *want* to meet him. Ever wonder what would happen to you if you lived alone in the woods for forty years? It's not a pretty picture."

"Thanks for the story, man. Guess I was lucky to get out of there alive."

"What about your bike?"

"I don't know," I said.

I lay back on my bed and thought about what it would be like to be a hermit in the woods. Part of me thought it wouldn't be that bad. No school. No people. Why not? With a good trail bike, a nice little cabin. Just ride to town once in a while for gas and supplies and spend the rest of the time doing whatever you wanted. It didn't sound like a bad life.

I found myself thinking about the hermit. Was he really crazy, or was it all made up? Maybe some people just wake up and realize the world is crazy and the only way to stay sane is to get away from all the craziness.

Chapter Three

I wasn't three steps off the bus when Anton noticed I was limping. "Fall off that piece of crap you ride?" he asked. "Or did it finally just fall apart underneath of you?"

I glared at him but didn't want to get into anything. "Yeah, I fell," I said. And I limped on. My leg hurt worse today. I wondered if I should go to a doctor.

But if my parents found out, I might never ride again. They had shown me pictures of motorcycle accidents and stories about kids getting hurt, even killed, on bikes. I tried to explain that all you had to do was use good judgement and not push the limits.

But, of course, I broke those two sacred rules all the time.

I turned and realized that Anton was right behind me. "When you feel better, you should come down to the pit with me and some of the boys. We can show you some stuff. It's wild down there." Anton's father owned a few dump trucks, bulldozers and front-end loaders. He hauled stone and gravel from a gravel pit on their property where Anton and his friends biked.

"Thanks, Anton. Maybe later."

"Yeah, later," he said and laughed. He was laughing at me. "I'll say hi to Sonia for you."

That was pure Anton. Right then I hated his guts. But I wasn't going to do a thing about it.

The rest of the week I limped from class to class. I didn't let my parents see me limp at home. The scrape on my leg looked ugly, but it was healing. My ribs still ached, but it was a dull ache.

At night I watched dirt-bike videos in my room and got depressed about losing my bike. I didn't have any money to get another bike. I'd have to get a part-time job. But that would mean working after school and weekends, the very times I'd want to be on my bike. And the only part-time job I knew of was working for Anton's rich old man. It was all pretty dismal.

Before I became fully conscious Saturday morning, I found myself being happy. Saturday. I'd hop on my bike and…That's when I really woke up and remembered.

I jumped out of bed and looked out my window. It was a beautiful day. And that made me mad.

I got dressed, found my backpack and threw a few things into it. I tromped downstairs and packed water and sandwiches—one peanut butter and jelly, one bologna.

My mom showed up just then. "What's up, Josh?"

"I'm going for a hike," I said.

"That's great. Anyone going with you?"

I thought about telling her Kyle was coming just to make her feel better. But I hated lying to my parents. "No. Just me."

"Can I pack you anything?"

"No. I'm good."

"Don't forget your cell phone."

"I've got it," I said. I unzipped a pouch to show her. The phone was there with my Swiss Army knife. I didn't point out that where I was going, the cell phone wouldn't be of much use.

She hugged me. "Be careful," she said. "Don't get lost." I knew that my parents worried, and they could tell that something was wrong this week.

Then I was out the door and walking down the street. The sky was blue. It was warm. My leg was stiff, but it was much better. My ribs only hurt if I took a deep breath or if I laughed. I doubted that I'd be doing much laughing.

I reckoned it would be a two-hour hike to get to where I'd dumped the bike. I tried jogging some of it, but that made my leg hurt. Eventually, I came to Loggerman Creek. I hadn't seen a soul all morning. And now the sky was overcast. I hoped it wasn't going to rain. I hadn't packed any rain gear.

I sat on a rock, ate half a bologna sandwich and wondered which way to go. They called him the hermit of Loggerman Creek. He must live near the creek. I followed the logging road north along the creek for another half hour. There was no sign of a shack or a hermit. When the trail went east again, I figured I would follow the creek. I couldn't see any sign of a footpath, but a hermit probably didn't want to lead anyone to his house.

I picked my way along the shoreline over the boulders and fallen trees. The air had turned cooler. Then it started to rain.

I was going to get soaked even if I turned around and headed home.

I cursed myself for not packing rain gear. How stupid could you get? I thought about giving up and going home. But I soldiered on.

About twenty minutes later, I saw a narrow footpath leading away from the creek. I decided to follow it. Water dripped down on me from the overhanging branches. I was starting to feel a chill. This was not good.

The trail had dwindled down to nearly nothing, but I smelled smoke. I followed my nose. This was a good way to get lost in a forest. But once I made my decision, I could see no turning back. It was wood-smoke for sure. Somebody was burning spruce in a woodstove.

I stopped when I saw the shack. It was a rough log cabin with one window and a door made of planks. The roof was covered with an old green tarp, and there was a small metal pipe for a chimney. It was small, probably one room.

I imagined it was dark and smelly inside. There was a distinct odor of old fish mixed with the smoke. Behind the cabin was a shed also made from logs with another tarp over the roof.

I was shivering and wet, but I was here. There was no turning back. I walked to the door and was about to knock when the hermit swung the door sharply open and stood inches from my face. "You!" he shouted at me.

I couldn't speak.

"What do you want?" he demanded.

"Give me back my dirt bike," I said.

He laughed. "No," he said.

"It's my property," I said. "You stole it."

"I found it lying in the woods."

"Where is it?" I demanded, but he could tell I was scared. My voice was shaking.

He closed the door on me, and I heard him slide a bolt, locking it.

I stood my ground.

"I called the cops," I lied.

Silence.

Then the door opened again. He looked scared. "You what?"

I was feeling weak now, and cold. I looked down at the ground. "No, I didn't."

"This is between you and me," he said angrily. "No one else."

The hermit picked up a long-handled ax that was leaning against the shack. "Follow me," he said.

He walked toward the shed. I thought about running, but my leg was hurting again. And the hermit knew these woods better than anyone. I wouldn't stand a chance. So I followed him.

When we got to the shed, he motioned with his ax. "Your noise toy is in there," he said. The rough plank door was latched from the outside. There were no windows in the shed. This did not look good. I stood and waited.

He raised the ax high over his head. With a grunt, he swung down hard, embedding the ax blade deeply into a chopping block. I nearly jumped out of my skin.

The hermit looked annoyed and shook his head. "Lost," he said. "All of you. Hopelessly lost."

He slowly opened the door and propped it back with a stick. He walked into the darkness of the shed and returned, wheeling my bike out into the rain.

I stared at it.

"You fixed my bike?" The front wheel was fine. The fork was straightened. The gas tank had the dents taken out as well. It was still scratched-up and ratty-looking, but the old guy had fixed my bike. I couldn't believe it.

"Uh-huh," he said. "And tuned it too. It was running terrible. You waste fuel that way. Ruin the planet. You should take better care."

His face was serious. I didn't know what to think.

"You cold?" he asked.

I was shaking.

"Wanna dry out?"

I nodded.

"I'll put her away till you're ready," he said, sounding like a kindly grandfather. He rolled the bike back into the shed and then led me to his cabin. "Xanadu," he said.

"Pardon me?"

"Xanadu. *X-A-N-A-D-U*. You pronounce the *X* like a *Z*. It's the name of my home. Every home should have a name. What do you call yours?"

"I don't know. Just home, I guess."

"See what I mean? You're all hopelessly lost," he said as I stepped into the semi-darkness of Xanadu.

As my eyes adjusted to the dim light, I looked at my bizarre surroundings. The log walls were shiny, as if they had been polished. The woodstove was not a stove at all but an old washing machine with the glass part of the door missing. Hanging from the rafters were dozens and dozens of fish and what looked like snakes.

"Eels, not snakes," he said as if reading my mind. "Stand by the fire. Dry out. Ever eat dried eels? Nothing like it." He grabbed one and offered it to me. He took down another and began to munch on it himself. "Lots of protein," he said. "Try it."

Chapter Four

I nibbled at the eel. It was disgusting.
The hermit laughed. "It's 'cause you're
used to store-bought food. This is the
real thing."

I smiled, handed him back the dried
eel and hovered over the washer-
woodstove for warmth. I watched him
strip the dry flesh off the bones. When
he finished eating the eel, he tossed the

remains into the fire. The room was quiet except for the sound of the logs burning and the rain pelting on the tarp.

"I'm sorry about the other day," I said. "You okay?"

He sort of snorted. "That was nothing. I've had much worse. Hurt my pride though, I guess. Lost my cool."

"How do you know about bikes?" I asked.

"I know about a lot of things," he said. "It's all up here." He pointed to his head. He paused, looked at me intently and scratched the hair on his bearded jaw. "So they say I'm crazy, do they?"

I shrugged, afraid to say the wrong thing.

"Maybe it's them that's crazy. The whole world is crazy. Maybe I'm the only one who is sane. Hmm." He walked to a shelf of books. "Let's look up the definition of sanity." He turned some pages. "Here it is. 'Soundness of mind.

Mental balance of health.'" He held the book out. "Look here. It's a picture of me by the definition."

I thought it was just a joke. But out of the pages of the dictionary he took out an old photo and handed it to me. It was a snapshot of a young man, not much older than me. I studied the face of the skinny young guy in the photo. Then it clicked. The eyes. "This is you."

"Was me. Back in the day, as they say."

Even though I was warming up, I shivered again. I found it impossible to connect the boy in the photo with the old man in front of me. I turned the photo over and it said simply, *Jonathan at 17*.

"My mother had elegant handwriting," was all he said.

"Jonathan," I said out loud.

"All three syllables. I don't let anyone call me John. You?"

"Pardon?"

"How many syllables in your name?"

"One."

"That's no good."

"Well, my full name is three. Josh-u-a."

"Like in the Old Testament." He turned to his bookshelf and grabbed a Bible. "Read it six times so far. Thinking about going at it again. Might have missed something."

"You religious?" I asked.

"Not really. Just like to read. I'll read anything I can get my hands on. Go down by the creek on a nice day with a good book—or a crummy one—and sit there and read. Makes me feel peaceful."

I had a million questions, but the thing that popped into my head was about the hundred men he'd killed. Maybe he really had kept count and then deserted. No, I wasn't going to go there.

It grew quiet again, and I realized the rain had let up.

"Which syllable?" he said.

"What?"

"Which of the three? Ooh? Do they call you Ooh? Or is it Ah? Either one sounds odd to my ear." The guy had a weird sense of humor.

"Josh. They call me Josh."

"In the Bible, Joshua was a rather fierce leader. You like that? Fierce, I mean?"

"Not really."

He studied my face in a way that made me uncomfortable. He was looking directly into my eyes. "No," he said, breathing a stench of dried eel in my face. "I don't see fierce. I see confused, but I also see determined."

"A little of both," I said. I inched away and looked up. "Rain's stopped. I should get going."

"Back to the land of the crazies?"

"You're right. There is a lot of craziness. A lot of things don't make sense."

"You got that one right."

I reached for the door, but in the dim light of the room I couldn't find the door handle. I felt a thrill of panic. Jonathan was walking toward me. Then his arm shot out quickly like he was going to push me into the wall. But he didn't touch me at all. He flipped a latch and the door opened.

"I'll get your bike," he said and walked quickly past me.

He rolled my old Kawasaki out of the shed and held it while I got on.

"Thanks for fixing my bike. It means a lot to me."

"I know," he said. "So take better care of it."

When I kicked it to start, it miraculously started right away. I was shocked. It idled smooth as silk. The old guy must really have tuned it up. "I will,"

I said. And as I was ready to split, I said, "I owe you one."

"Yes, you do. Can I put in my request now?"

"Sure."

"Bring me a five-pound bag of brown rice. And a book. Any book."

I gave him a thumbs-up.

"And one more thing. Don't mention this to anyone."

I nodded, let out the clutch and eased away slowly, threading the bike through the trees. It wasn't until I got back on the logging road that I realized I didn't have my helmet—another promise to my parents broken. I decided to take it easy on the way home.

Chapter Five

It was just my luck to be coming out of the woods as Anton was roaring down the street. His Yamaha was the loudest I'd ever heard. It was an amazing red firecracker of a bike. I should have hung back on the trail and just let him go by. I don't know what got into me. I raced out of the ditch at the end of the trail and shot out in front of Anton. He had to swerve to avoid me. It was a truly stupid thing to do.

Then I let up on the gas and headed home. I should have known Anton wouldn't think this was funny. I heard him make a quick U-turn and head back toward me. He pulled up alongside and nodded toward the side of the road. I pulled over.

He yanked off a helmet with a dark faceplate. It looked like something an astronaut would wear. Then he turned off his engine. I did the same.

"Riding without a helmet," he said. "And harassing the public."

I immediately regretted my actions. Why didn't I just let him ride by?

"Just fooling around," I said, trying to make light of it.

I thought he was going to get really pissed off. Instead, he smiled. There was something about the smile that made me angry. It was like he was laughing at me.

"Good," he said. "I like fooling around on bikes. It's what I live for. I'm headed to the gravel pit. Nobody's working there today. Why don't you join me?"

I shook my head. "Nah. Like you say, I don't have my helmet. And I gotta get home."

"Not up for a little challenge, you and that pile of junk?"

I gave a look that conveyed what I thought of him, but I didn't say anything. I kick-started my bike and began to ride off slowly. I heard Anton's bike fire up with a raspy roar. He pulled directly into my path, and I had to jerk hard to the right and skid to a stop. "What?" I said.

"Tomorrow then. At the pit. One o'clock. A little one-on-one." The words were innocent enough, but it was the way he said them. I'd had kids taunt me all my life. I had learned not to let them get to me.

But I found I couldn't do that. "Sure," I said. "I could use the exercise."

My dad was in the front yard, and he watched me pull the bike into the shed. "Josh," he said as I walked to the house, "you're not supposed to ride without your helmet. That was the deal."

"I'm really sorry. I forgot it. I won't let it happen again."

"Sorry doesn't cut it this time," he said. "Your bike is grounded for a week."

"But…"

"We had a deal. You broke it. No helmet: no bike."

I didn't say anything more. How could I explain? This was so unfair.

That night we ate dinner in nearly complete silence. I don't think my dad told my mom about the helmet, because she would have been mad too. She might insist I get rid of the bike. I guess my dad was doing me a favor. I needed to keep a low profile, be good and get back on my bike in a week.

Except I had a problem. Anton. He'd make a fool out of me at school if I didn't show.

Saturday night I read motorcycle magazines and dreamed about a road trip in the wilderness for days and days. I'd camp and have the world to myself.

My cell phone rang. It was Sonia.

"Hey, Josh."

"Hey, Sonia."

"Anton told me you're going to the pit tomorrow."

"I guess so," I said, sounding like a wimp.

"I want you to be careful," she said.

This was strange. This was the girl who had been acting like I no longer existed. "Why?" I asked.

There was a pause. "Well, Anton was talking about it. It seems you really ticked him off."

"Doesn't take much to tick off Anton."

"I know. He can be a jerk."

"Then why do you like him?" I asked.

"I don't know. He's interesting, I guess," she said matter-of-factly. That was more like Sonia. Liking a guy who acts like an egomaniac because he was "interesting."

I didn't say anything. There was another awkward pause.

"Look," she finally said, "it's just that he said he was going to make you eat dirt."

"That's just a biking term."

"Yeah, but he seemed like he was going to try to hurt you. Push you too far. Something."

"I already knew that."

"Look, I just don't want to see you get hurt," she said, sounding sweet.

"Thanks," I said.

"Bye."

The girl must have still had some feelings for me if she didn't want to see me get wasted. I didn't know how I was going to get to the pit tomorrow with my parents hovering, but I had no choice.

Anton was going to eat dirt, not me.

Chapter Six

I may have been a no-show for the Sunday
challenge, but my parents decided to visit
friends who lived a two-hour drive away.
They left after lunch. My father did not
verbally remind me about the bike, but
he held his index finger up to my face.
I knew what he meant.

My Kawasaki started like a dream.
"Thank you, Jonathan," I said out loud.

I would ask him to teach me about tuning a bike. How did a guy who had lived in the woods for forty years know about tuning a motorcycle engine?

I heard Anton's bike and some other two-stroke motorbikes before I turned off the road to the gravel pit. The gate was open, and I drove down the rutted driveway and studied what lay before me. The pit was a massive scar on the land, for sure. Anton's father had been hauling gravel, stones and dirt out of here for ten years or more. The place must have been twenty acres—a wasteland. In the middle were four giant mounds of loose stone, sand and gravel. The sides of the pit were over forty feet tall and were near vertical. I wondered how this was allowed. Can you just buy a chunk of land, cut down the trees and sell it until there was nothing left but bedrock? Was that legal? Obviously the answer to both questions was yes.

Two of Anton's friends were here. I saw Billy's jazzed-up Honda and Deano's Suzuki, and Anton was on his Yamaha. Anton was working a controlled fishtailing run through an area that was all sand. Then he, followed by his friends, launched up one of the smaller mounds of gravel.

I'd been here on my bike before. I sneaked in a few evenings just before dark and tried my hand at this game. It was sure different than biking in the forest. It gave me a thrill, but it just wasn't me. Riding a trail in the woods was all about the unexpected challenges and what I liked to call creative control.

This was raw, push-your-bike-to-the-limits power thrashing.

I waited for Anton to spot me. When he did, he and Billy and Deano all wrenched their accelerators with a twist of their wrists and sped toward me.

Billy and Deano just nodded. Anton flipped up his faceplate so I could see the evil grin on his ugly face. "Surprised you came," he said.

"Nothing better to do," I countered.

"When's the last time you climbed?"

"It's been a while," I said.

"We'll go easy on you," he lied.

"What's the deal?"

"You do whatever I do," said Anton.

"And?"

"And nothing," he said. "Just trying to prove a point."

"And the point is?"

Anton laughed. This was all to make me look bad. Make me feel like a loser. It was that simple.

Anton didn't answer. He flipped his faceplate down and headed for the first mound. I tightened my chin strap, revved the engine and raced after him. I gave it as much speed as I could across the floor of the pit, then downshifted as I climbed the first hill. I was unaccustomed to the loose sand and stone beneath me. I hunched forward, tight to my bike, trying to keep my back wheel from slipping too far sideways. The dust cloud from Anton's bike was just ahead of me. I wasn't exactly right behind him, but I was holding my own.

I didn't realize I was near the top, but suddenly my front wheel was chewing air. I nearly lost it as I started to descend with my throttle open way too wide. My hands barely hanging on to the grips. I shifted my weight to the back of the bike and braked with too much pressure on the front brake. The rear of the bike lifted off the ground, and I was sure I was about to flip over the handlebars. I eased up on the front brake and slowed by downshifting all the way to first. I skidded sideways and I was down, my injured leg grinding against the loose stones.

But instinct kicked in. Or maybe my bike saved me. It righted itself, and I found myself carving back into a controlled descent. Not fast now. Just controlled.

When I got down onto the flat, Anton was waiting.

"You're a little rough around the edges," Anton said.

"Just getting warmed up," I said.

"Ready?"

I nodded.

The second hill was higher. And more difficult. There were sections of pure sand. My bike didn't really have the tires or the power for this, but I fish-tailed my way upward. I didn't like it. I felt like I was bullying my bike. Not a good thing. Then there was a section of scree that you had to jimmy across on an angle. There was no way to get traction going straight up on the loose stones. At the top I was ready for the front wheel to kiss air. I readjusted my balance and my speed without a touch on the front brake. I was over the top.

I was pleased with myself and ready to take on the third and highest of the mounds when Anton raced off in a another direction. He headed toward the south wall of the gravel pit and turned off his bike.

I caught up with him, turned off my bike and took my helmet off for a gulp of fresh air.

He nodded at the carved wall of the pit. It was the height of a four-story building and much steeper than the dirt mounds.

"Whaddaya think?" Anton asked.

Billy and Deano were here now. They reminded me of vultures. Billy pulled out his cell phone and took a picture of me. I guess I looked a little shaken. The name of the game, after all, was humiliation.

Something in me snapped. I decided to go first. I strapped my helmet into place, and lit up the bike, heading away from the wall of the pit. I figured they'd all think I chickened out. Billy was probably capturing a video clip of me on the run. If so, I hope he got the part where I powered into my one-eighty and raced back at them full throttle.

I should have known better. My bike didn't have the power for such a steep climb. But Anton had gotten to me. I floored it straight toward Anton, who was still hovering over his Yamaha. I squeezed between him and Billy. And I do mean squeezed. You should have seen the look on their faces.

As I approached the steep edge of the pit wall, I noticed that there were no tire tracks on the face of it. No one had been practicing here. Maybe no one had ever tried such an impossible climb.

But it was too late to reconsider.

I hunched forward, geared down and climbed. The engine never faltered, even though I was pushing the bike too hard. Halfway up the climb, the sane part of my brain told me to bail.

I wasn't looking up though, and I wasn't looking down. I put my trust in the sound of the engine giving everything it had. I was certain this was way too steep. There was no way I was going to make it. I was about to flip backward and go ass over handlebars down the embankment. Just when I thought I had lost it for sure, I was over the top. I had made it.

As the front tire came down on horizontal ground, I wasn't at all prepared. The rear wheel dug in, and I didn't cut the throttle quick enough. I veered sharp to the left and came down on my uninjured leg. The bike was spinning around as if it wanted to pull me back down over the edge.

I killed the engine and assessed the damage.

I stood up. Nothing hurt. I picked up my bike. It looked okay.

Then I tried to remember how to breathe.

I popped off my helmet and smiled down at the three other bikers, shocked at how far down they were. They hadn't started the climb yet.

I just stood there for a minute, letting my heart slow down. Billy and Deano looked like they were saying something to Anton. Why wasn't he going for it?

Then it clicked. They had planned to lure me into doing the wall. They had tricked me into going first. And I fell for it. Anton had no intention of doing it himself.

Billy and Deano stayed put, but Anton put on his helmet and started to ride. I wanted to shout something, but I didn't. I wondered what the story would be at school now. But I knew it would be lies.

Anton stopped. He fiddled with some-thing on his bike, and then he turned and raced toward me. He had decided to go for it.

Because I was so high up, it all looked like slow motion. I heard Deano yell, "Don't do it!" I watched Anton hit the steep climb and power higher and higher. At first it looked like he was going to make it. But I think all that extra power was working against him. He couldn't control the bike on some-thing this steep.

He lost it about three-quarters of the way up.

And I mean really lost it.

Just as the front wheel came free of the hill and the bike started to flip over backward, Anton let go and threw himself off to the side. He clawed at the stones and dirt as the bike tumbled downward. Anton kept grabbing at the dirt to slow his descent, but it wasn't pretty.

His bike stalled and bounced off a couple of rocks on the way down, landing in a smashed-up pile at the bottom. Anton had good instinct. He kept clawing at the side of the hill as he slid until he made it to the bottom. After a few seconds, he stood up, and I could tell he wasn't seriously injured.

The he threw his helmet on the ground. As Billy and Deano came to help him, he walked to his truly mangled bike and let out a loud curse. His words were like music to my ears. "My father's gonna kill me."

The forest looked peaceful and inviting. I saw a path that would lead to the logging road. I started up my bike, and it purred like a kitten. I gently eased onto the path and headed home.

Chapter Seven

My bike was back in the shed, and I was washed and presentable when my parents returned. They weren't even suspicious. Once I realized I had gotten away with that, I vowed I'd leave the bike alone for the rest of the week.

I wondered if Deano or Billy would tell other kids what had happened at the pit. I had bragging rights, but I wasn't going to use them. At school I kept expecting someone to at least ask me what happened, but no one did.

Despite her Saturday night phone call, Sonia had avoided me on Monday and Tuesday. I finally saw her Wednesday. "Thanks again for the heads-up," I said quietly.

She looked straight ahead as we walked.

"What?" I asked.

"You didn't have to go and do what you did," she said angrily.

"What did I do?"

"Sabotaged Anton's bike. Billy said you put something in the gas."

I was stunned. "That's a lie."

She stopped. "Well, Anton's bike is mangled. How do you explain that?"

"He challenged me. I beat him. He pushed his limits and got wasted. It wasn't my idea, and I didn't do anything to his bike."

She didn't believe me. "I feel like I betrayed him," she said. And then she walked away.

I wanted to find Deano and Billy and kick them both in the head. I wanted to confront Anton. I was so mad.

But I didn't. I knew that whatever I said or did, Anton would make me look bad. It wouldn't be hard with Billy and Deano to back him up. So, instead, I went to class and fumed. I thought about Jonathan as I sat through history class. And I thought, yeah, maybe I'll move out in the woods and become a hermit like him. Then I won't have to deal with this crap.

I left school quickly to avoid Anton. I didn't trust myself. I actually ran out the front door. If I couldn't bike today, maybe running would help. I thought about going to see Jonathan. I felt like he was my only friend now. But it was too far, and I didn't have enough daylight.

When I was three blocks from school, I phoned Kyle on my cell.

"Josh," he said. "What do you have, like, an evil twin or something?"

"You heard the story that Anton's spreading?"

"What was it? Sugar?"

"It was nothing. I did nothing. I beat the creep, fair and square."

There was a pause. "I believe you," he said. "I really do. But no one else does."

"I don't really care," I said. "But Kyle, you said there were ATVers who are friends with the hermit. Who are they?"

"Um, Carl Wilson for one. And Gabe's father, Dwight. Oh, and Dave Jenkins, who works at the hardware store."

"Thanks, Kyle. Thanks a lot." I hung up.

Dave Jenkins was standing behind a counter at the back of the store. He was a cheerful middle-aged man with a messy head of hair. I introduced myself and told him about my encounter with Jonathan. At first he seemed wary.

"You weren't harassing him last month?"

"No, why? What happened?"

"Some teenage kids went back there on a Friday night on four-wheelers and tried to scare the poor guy. They had big lights and were shining them into his shack. Jonathan had heard them coming, of course. He was up in a tree. I guess he got fed up with them and jumped out of the tree and scared the crap out of them. Still, it shook him up. He doesn't like anyone invading his privacy."

"I can understand that."

"You say he fixed your bike?"

"Yeah. I couldn't believe it."

"He must like you. He doesn't trust many people."

"Neither do I," I said. "But is he… okay?"

"Depends on what you mean by okay. He still thinks that if he leaves the woods he'll be arrested."

"For deserting?"

"Yeah. But that's not going to happen. Vietnam is long over. And he did what a man had to do. He walked away from a dirty war."

"But not before he killed a hundred men."

"I don't know if anyone kept count. He was a soldier though. It was his job."

"You've known him for a long time, right?" I asked.

"Yep. Me and Dwight and Carl. We take supplies out to him sometimes. Flour, rice. Basic stuff."

"What could I do to help him?"

"He doesn't like people fussing over him. But if he's already let you in his shack, he must think you're okay. But Josh, I gotta warn you. He's unpredictable—scared silly of anyone in a uniform. And helicopters. He goes nuts if he even hears a helicopter. Something to do with the war, I guess."

"Thanks for the information."

"Get to know him. But don't talk about him to other kids. He's been out in those woods for forty years. People, if they think about him at all, think he's a freak. But they leave him alone. That's what he needs." Dave paused. "But he could use a friend. And maybe you're it. But you gotta be a friend on his terms."

"Got it. Thanks."

Dave smiled and looked at me. "Did he offer you any eel?"

"Yep."

He smiled wider. "Did you eat it?"

"Tried."

"You'll get used to it," he said.

Chapter Eight

I didn't ride my bike for the rest of the week. My parents were happy. The rumor about me pouring sugar in Anton's gas tank found its way to my mom.

"You wouldn't do a thing like that, would you?" she asked.

"Of course not," I told her. But I could tell by her frown that she wasn't convinced. And that really ticked me off. I couldn't believe that my own mother would think I'd do such a thing.

While I washed the dishes Thursday evening, I asked my father, "Is it Sunday or Saturday that I'm allowed back on my bike?"

"Well, technically Sunday, but I guess you can have it for the weekend."

Friday I went to the store and bought five pounds of brown rice, a bag of potatoes, cooking oil and flour. Basics. Just what a hermit might need. I also fixed up my bike—cleaned the dust out of the air filter, washed the bike and even touched up some of the scratches.

First thing Saturday morning, I left a note for my sleeping parents, got on the bike with the supplies strapped behind me and headed into the woods. It felt so good to be back on my bike. Every inch of me felt alive.

I passed a couple of men in camouflage jackets on ATVs with racks holding rifles. Hunting season had started. This was not good news for someone who likes to hang out in the woods. And there was one other kid on a two-stroke Suzuki that was spewing smoke. I let them pass me so that no one was around when I pulled off-trail toward Jonathan's shack. I even stopped and went back to cover up my tracks. I didn't think Jonathan would appreciate other visitors.

I pulled up to the cabin and turned off my bike. At first it seemed like nobody was around. I knocked on the door. Nothing.

I sat down on a strange-looking chair made from alder branches woven together and lashed with strips of bark. It was obvious the hermit had built it.

About an hour passed and then I heard something move behind me. I turned around and there he was. He had a handful of some kind of roots. He stared at me like he didn't know who I was.

"Hi, Jonathan," I said.

He squinted, and I realized that there must be something wrong with his eyesight.

"Joshua," he finally said. "I was beginning to think I had made you up. I imagine things sometimes."

"No, I'm real."

"Did you see any hunters?" he asked warily.

"Yeah. Two guys on a four-wheeler. Back on the trail."

"I don't like hunters. The guns, you know. And they kill things they don't eat."

"How come they are allowed to hunt here?" I asked. "I thought it was some kind of wildlife preserve."

"That's the government for ya. They preserve the wild living things for the hunters to kill. Those are the kind of rules governments come up with." He squinted again.

"You okay?" I asked.

He shook his head. "Can't see as good as I used to. Getting old, I guess."

I grabbed the pack off my bike and handed it to him. "Supplies," I said. He didn't open the pack right away. He looked stunned. "Check it out. I hope it's stuff you can use."

He slowly undid the straps and looked in. Then he set the pack on the ground and took out the five pounds of rice. A monster grin crept over his face. "How'd you know it was my birthday?"

I wondered for a minute and then decided not to say, *I didn't*. Maybe it really was his birthday. Maybe not. I let him have his moment. He lifted out the potatoes. "Spuds. Haven't had spuds in a year. I've been eating these instead," he said, pointing at the roots he had gathered, now laying on the ground. "Indian cucumber, it's called. It's all right but not the same. Some nights I wake up dreaming that I'm frying potatoes in a pan. I can even smell them cooking."

He continued to look at each item in a kind of wonder, moving his hands around the square bottle of corn oil and weighing the bag of flour. And then he sat down on the ground and began to cry.

I didn't know what to do. So I did nothing. After a few minutes of sobbing, Jonathan stood up. He looked embarrassed. He blinked a couple of times and said, "There, I think I can see better now." I think he was joking. He motioned for me to sit back down in his homemade chair. He sat down on a log.

There were rifle shots—hunters. But they were a long way off. Jonathan's eyes darted away, but then he looked straight at me.

"When you kill a man with your bare hands, your hands are never the same again," he said. "And you have to look at those hands for the rest of your life. That's the hard part."

"This was the war?"

"I never should have gone. Worst of it was, I was good at it." There was another gun shot. And another. "Guess I was like them." He nodded toward the gunfire. "It's easy to kill a living thing, even a man, from a distance. You aim, fire, walk away. But I ended up in a foxhole. Thought no one was there. And there was the enemy. Face-to-face finally. No room to shoot. All I could do was put my hands on his throat. No time to think. It wasn't until he was dead that I realized he was just a kid." He paused. "Your age." We heard another three shots and someone yelling in triumph. I wondered what they had killed.

"I'm sorry," I said. "It wasn't your fault."

"Yes, it was. All I wanted to do was run and hide."

"That was all a long time ago, right?"

"I was married, you know," he said.

"No, I didn't know that."

"When I finally made it back home, she said I should turn myself in. But I couldn't do that. So I ran. I came here." He swallowed. "And never left."

He had a far-off look now. "You okay?" I asked.

"Everything went out of focus and dim again," he said. Then he shrugged. "But I guess I'm getting old."

"How often is this happening?"

He swallowed and tried to focus on me again, but it was like he was seeing right through me. "It was like once a month before. Now it's a couple of times a day."

I thought about it for a minute. There was a doctor in town. An old guy, kind of quirky and retired. "Jonathan, why don't you let me ride you into town so you could get checked out by a doctor?"

He stood bolt upright, and a look of panic came over him. He stepped back and stumbled a little. "No," was all he said. "Now go." He turned and went into his cabin. I heard him lock the latch.

Chapter Nine

It took a couple of trips back to Jonathan before he accepted me again. I told him I wasn't going to take him to a doctor. I brought him more food and even multivitamins. I had read on the Internet that kids in poor countries have failing eyesight from a lack of vitamin A. It was likely that Jonathan was missing some things in his diet, so what the heck.

I handed him the bottle of vitamins and told him to see if they helped his eyesight.

"I don't take drugs," he said.

"These are vitamins, that's all."

"Manufactured?"

"Well, yes. I guess so."

"I don't trust the companies that make them. You don't know what could be in there."

"True. But trust me on this." I cracked the seal on the cap, opened it and popped one in my mouth. "They're chewable," I said. "Tastes like oranges. Well, sort of like oranges." I handed him the bottle and he studied it.

Then we sat in silence for over ten minutes. I had learned not to push things.

Eventually he put the vitamins in his coat pocket and pointed up at the sky. "You believe in UFOS?"

"Maybe. You?"

"Yeah. I think they're up there protecting us."

"How?"

"I don't know," he said. "I just think they are watching us. I think that they watch all the terrible things people do and wish they could stop all the hurting. But they can't."

"You've had contact with them?"

He shrugged. "Not really. I see things moving in the sky at night. I'm pretty sure the aliens are smarter than us and friendly. I think they step in when things get too bad and prevent us from blowing up the whole world."

It was crazy talk, for sure, but who was I to say he was wrong. "Good thing they're up there then."

He nodded. "But they're sad. Real sad. They wish they could help more."

"Yep. We could use all the help we could get."

"You betcha." He blinked hard and then took the vitamins out, unscrewed the lid, popped one in his mouth and chewed.

"Hmm. Like candy," he said.

"You like candy?"

"No." But he chewed and swallowed anyway. Then he got to his feet. I was afraid I had scared him again somehow. "C'mon. Gotta show you something."

I followed him to the shed. He went inside, and when he came back out, my jaw dropped.

He was rolling out a really old stripped-down motorcycle.

And there was a big smile on his face. It was a crazy smile, for sure, but I was getting used to that.

"No way!"

"Oh yeah. It's how I got here. This was my father's. He wanted me to turn myself in too. Instead, I stole his motorcycle and rode it here. It's a nineteen forty-nine Harley. A classic."

"It's a monster," I said. "A beautiful monster. Does it still work?"

Jonathan straddled it and kicked the starter. It fired up immediately. The sound of the engine was deep but soft. I'd never heard such a quiet bike. He closed his eyes for a second.

And then he turned if off. "I don't ride it much anymore. When I left my wife and my hometown and got on this bike, I decided I would ride it until the road ended and the forest began. And I'd go as deep into that forest as I could, park the bike and live there. Alone. And that's what I did."

I tried to picture a younger version of the old hermit on a Harley—no helmet, the wind in his hair. I thought about how hard it must have been to leave everything behind. He must have felt the whole world had turned against him.

"Farther to the north, there's an old road that miners once used. It must have connected to the outside world at one point. A big section of trees blocks the road now. It begins and ends in the middle of the forest. Sometimes I go up there."

"Could we do that together sometime? I'd follow you on my bike."

"Maybe," he said. "Maybe. But winter's coming. Might not be many good days left, and I'm saving my last can of gas. Just in case…" He didn't seem to want to finish the sentence, and I knew better than to ask.

Chapter Ten

I headed out to Xanadu again the next day. It was getting colder and the days were shorter. The ground was frozen hard, and riding the trail was more like riding pavement.

I helped Jonathan haul dead trees to his shack, cut them with a big-toothed saw and split some logs with his ultra-sharp ax. The wood was stacked both in the house and in the shed. He told me that he now took a vitamin every day. He said he still had some "fuzzy eyesight now and again," but it wasn't as bad as before. "Guess I should call you the doctor from now on," he said.

One Sunday, Dave Jenkins, along with Dwight and Carl, showed up on their four-wheelers. They had supplies for Jonathan. Jonathan built a fire, and Dave brought out a six-pack of beer. He gave a can to each of his buddies and one to Jonathan. I could tell they'd played this scene before.

Jonathan popped the tab on the can and then swallowed the contents in a single long pull. He crushed the can and handed it back to Dave with a smile on his face. Dave gave him a second can, and Jonathan did the same with it. Then he looked at me and saw the concern on my face. "Don't worry, kid. Two's my limit," he said.

The other men took their time drinking their beers. "Ready for winter, Jonathan?" Dwight asked.

"Ready as I'll ever be," he said. "The doc here helped me with firewood and fixing the place up a bit." I had thought the pipes to his stove looked too thin to be safe so I found some stovepipe in our attic and took it out to him.

The men nodded their approval. "We brought you the usual," Dave said.

"Much appreciated," Jonathan said.

"No sweat," said Dave. "Hunters giving you any grief?"

"Nope. They keep their distance." Jonathan didn't like hunters, even though he snared rabbits too.

"The forestry people wanted to let you know they're doing a survey of the tree growth. They'll be flying all over here soon—just routine stuff, but they wanted you to know."

Jonathan's eyes began to dart back and forth. "I hate helicopters," he said.

Dwight changed the subject. "How's that tarp working out? Keeping water out?"

"Yep." I was used to the squalor of the shack. But the tarp on the roof seemed like a primitive arrangement—especially during winter.

Dave must have been thinking the same thing I was. "We could rent a generator, haul some tools out here and build you a new cabin some day."

Jonathan shook his head. "No, I couldn't let you do that. This is my home. Be it ever so humble." And then he did a strange thing. He proceeded to recite a poem.

"To thee I'll return, overburdened
     with care;

The heart's dearest solace will
    smile on me there;
No more from that cottage again
    will I roam;
Be it ever so humble, there's no
    place like home.
Home, home, sweet, sweet, home!
There's no place like home, oh,
    there's no place like home!"

The men did not look surprised. "Two beer and he always recites a poem," Dave said. This was a side of Jonathan I'd never seen. He looked much calmer now.

"When did you learn that?" I asked.

"Oh. Long time ago. So long it doesn't even seem like it was in this lifetime. The author was John Howard Payne. I learned it in school, I guess. I liked books. Planned to become a high-school English teacher."

"No way!" I said. There was so much about Jonathan I didn't know.

"It's true. Then the war mucked things up. I got drafted before I ever set foot in a university classroom."

I heard motorbikes in the distance, and everyone grew quiet. Dave put the small fire out by shoveling dirt onto it. I recognized the unmistakable sound of Anton's repaired bike and two others. Jonathan closed his eyes and his lips moved, but he didn't say anything out loud. Soon it became clear that the bikes were not coming this way. I secretly wished that Anton would hit a patch of ice so he could put a few new dents in his machine. We listened as the noise of the bike engines faded in the distance.

"Gonna snow this week for sure," Dave finally said, breaking the silence.

"The birds tell me it's gonna be a real wicked winter," Jonathan added. And then he smiled and let out a whistle through the space between his front teeth.

Chapter Eleven

Dave was right. It did snow. The first big blast of the year. I worried about Jonathan, although I reminded myself that he'd survived out there for forty years. He had firewood. I'd help change his stovepipes. He had supplies.

The snow stayed around for over two weeks. There was no way I could ride out to visit the hermit.

Dave Jenkins gave me a part-time job at the hardware store. It was mostly loading lumber and bags of stove pellets into people's cars. After two weeks I had enough money to buy spiked snow tires for my bike. I'd noticed the helicopters doing their survey, and I was worried about Jonathan out there in the forest all alone. Was he freaking out every time one came close? Was he having flashbacks to Vietnam?

Part of me identified with Jonathan. Some of us truly don't fit in with the rest of society. I was one of those people.

I could see why someone might want to ride into the woods on a stripped-down Harley and just chill for...well, forty years? And I couldn't even begin to imagine the horrors of a jungle war.

It was alternating between snow and sunshine on Saturday. But my new tires were great, and I had a snowmobile suit and winter boots. There was supposed to be a big snowfall, but the storm wouldn't pick up until the afternoon. If the snow got really deep, it wouldn't matter how good my snow tires were. Even now it was going to be tough traveling through the woods on two wheels. But I had to check on Jonathan.

I bundled up, packed some food, left a note for my folks and rolled the bike out of the shed. I noticed a helicopter passing over, heading toward the forest.

My road was icy from the compacted snow. Even with the studded tires, I felt the bike slide around under me. It was better in the forest, but the trail had been used by snowmobilers so there were deep ruts and icy spots. I took it real easy.

The forest seemed completely unfamiliar to me with everything covered in snow. I stopped a couple of times just to look around. When I turned off the engine, there was a beautiful silence unlike anything I remembered.

Birch trees hung over, weighted down with snow. The sun filtered through the bare frozen branches of the hardwood trees. I took a few deep breaths, feeling good to be alive.

I thought I was close to where I'd need to turn off the trail to find Jonathan's cabin. But with the forest floor covered in snow, I wasn't sure. There were no footprints in the snow to follow either. I got off my bike and paced up and down along the trail, hoping to see something to remind me of the way to his cabin. No luck.

I decided to do what I had done the first time. Where the road veered away from the creek, I took my bike off-trail and followed the bank, picking my way slowly through the soft snow. Twice I disturbed snow clinging to spruce boughs. I got dumped on each time, and snow found its way down my back and gave me chills.

Lesley Choyce

And then I saw the hermit's cabin.

But something was wrong.

There was no smoke coming from the chimney.

I revved the bike and plowed through yet more snow to get to the cabin. I threw off my helmet and parked the bike, but the kickstand wouldn't hold and it fell over. I left it.

The door to the shack was open.

"Jonathan!" I yelled. Was he out in the woods somewhere? Maybe he was hiding. Maybe he'd heard the bike and didn't know it was me.

I walked around the outside of the cabin first, figuring that if he was home, the fire would be burning. There would be smoke coming from the chimney. I yelled for him a couple more times, but there was no answer.

I walked into the cabin. It took a minute for my eyes to adjust to the dim light. And then I saw him.

Jonathan was lying on the floor with a long gash in his leg. There was a pool of blood on the rough boards of the floor.

He'd lost a lot of blood. I was scared and not at all sure what to do. But I had to do something. The room was cold. The door was open, and the fire in the stove was out. I leaned over him to hear if he was breathing. My heart was racing so fast that I couldn't hear anything else. I had to put my ear right up to his mouth. He smelled really bad. I had never gotten used to that. I held my breath and steadied myself. And then, yes, I detected it. He was breathing, but it was very light, very shallow.

He'd been like this for a long time, I was sure. He must have lost a lot of blood. I had to stop the bleeding somehow, and wasn't sure how. I reached inside my snowsuit and yanked off my leather belt. I'd taken a first-aid course a long time ago. I remembered being warned that if you put a tourniquet on, you couldn't undo it until the victim was safely in a hospital.

I had no idea how I was going to get Jonathan to a hospital. The gash was deep and long. An animal? I wondered. A bear? The cut was awful. My head felt light, and I thought I was going to throw up. I'd never seen anything like this in my life.

I decided to bandage the wound and try to stop the bleeding. A tourniquet might be too dangerous. I tore off the snowsuit and ripped off my shirt, then wrapped it around Jonathan's leg, tying the arms together to hold it in place. The blood soaked through, but it began to slow down. I gently moved Jonathan's legs away from the bloody mess on the floor. He groaned but did not wake up. Again I wondered what could have done this. That's when I heard the helicopter.

I ran outside and started waving my arms as the chopper flew over. I yelled and waved, but I was sure the pilot couldn't see me. The hermit's cabin was well hidden in the trees. I pulled up my snowmobile suit and decided to run to the creek. If the helicopter came back and I was on a rock in the middle of the creek, he'd see me. I hoped they were doing back and forth sweeps as part of their work. It was all I could think of.

I ran through the snow toward the water, falling several times, getting out of breath, but I could still hear the engine. As I approached Loggerman Creek, I could tell the helicopter was coming back this way. The noise of the engine and the whirring blades grew louder. My lungs were burning from running so hard in the cold.

The rocks at the edge of the creek were coated with ice. I slipped once and came down hard on my chin. I tasted blood.

But I got up and tried to make my way from one ice-covered boulder to the next toward the middle of the creek. There was ice all around—on the rocks, on fallen trees. Everything was slippery. And the water was maybe up to my stomach. The current was raging. I had almost made it to my destination—a big boulder in the middle of the creek. If I could only get there and start waving, there'd be a chance.

That's when I lost my footing and fell headfirst into the ice-cold water. The current began to drag me under. It was so cold, that I felt like I was being stabbed with sharp knives. I came up gasping for air and feeling angry at my failure. But I didn't give up. I pushed against the current and dragged myself up on the boulder. Shivering now, I planted my feet wide and threw my arms up into the air. I could hear the helicopter coming closer and closer.

But then suddenly the sound began to diminish. He was moving away. I couldn't believe it.

I waited for several desperate minutes, hoping the pilot would turn for another sweep. But it didn't happen. The only sound was the river gurgling around me. I was wet and shivering. My snowmobile suit was soaked through, and it was heavy. I felt a cramp in my leg. I had to get myself out of the creek and back to the cabin.

I lumbered back to the shore, walking through the bitterly cold water, arms outstretched to grab on to something if I fell. My legs barely worked. I inched forward and crawled on all fours up onto the slippery rocks of the shore.

Then, feeling frozen, heavy and defeated, I stumbled through the trees and snow. I was panting heavily when I reached the cabin. As I entered, I closed the door behind me. Jonathan was still unconscious, but the bleeding had stopped.

I tried to control my shivering, but I couldn't. It was beginning to sink in how bad this situation was. And I had only made things worse. I tore off my snowmobile suit. I had to get a fire going. I could feel my muscles tightening. In the dim light of the cabin, I searched frantically for matches.

I found them in the middle of a wooden table. A box of long wooden matches from the supplies I had brought in the fall. I saw a plastic bucket filled with birch bark and kindling near the stove. I lifted the lid of the makeshift rig and dropped in a handful of birch bark. Shaking fiercely now, I piled some kindling on it as best I could and lit the birch bark. As the fire started I added more kindling and a couple of larger pieces of wood. The fire roared to life, and I closed the lid.

I hovered over the fire for several long minutes, absorbing the warmth and trying to figure out what to do next.

I stripped off my wet clothes and pulled my cell phone out of my pants pocket. It had gone in the creek with me, but it had not been on. I found a grimy towel hanging on a nail. I dried myself and then gingerly dried the cell phone. It looked damp but not damaged.

I found an old flannel shirt, some torn jeans and wool socks and I put them on.

Jonathan let out a long moan. I felt weak and helpless. I stared at the cell phone and thought that yet a miracle would happen. I would turn it on and it would work. And I would somehow get a signal.

I flipped it open. Amazingly it still worked.

But there was no signal. I knew that on a good summer day, it would be a hard half-hour ride back toward town before I could get that. And with the snow, it would take much longer.

I couldn't let the fire go out, and I couldn't chance leaving here for help that may be hours away. I had no choice but to stay.

Chapter Twelve

I moved Jonathan onto his bed. I studied the wound on his leg. My shirt had sopped up a lot of blood, and I was fairly certain my first-aid training had told me not to remove it. Just leave it until he could be taken to a hospital. I covered him with blankets, studied his ragged breathing and looked at his ancient creased face.

More than anything I ever wanted in my life, I wanted this old guy to live. Outside, it began to snow. I thought again about trying to make a run for it on the bike to get help, but then he said something. It was a hiss at first and then a mumble. "Don't leave me," he whispered. "Don't leave me alone."

I walked over to him, expecting to see him awake, but his eyes were closed. "Can you hear me?" I said.

He nodded.

"Can I get you anything?"

"Water."

I got him some water from a jug, and then I sat by him for a few minutes. He faded into sleep or unconsciousness, and I felt very alone again.

I had to figure out what to do next. The fire was stoked. Jonathan had plenty of firewood. We'd stay warm. Then I remembered my bike fallen over outside in the snow. I might need it at some point. I found an old pair of rubber boots, put them on and went outside. The snow was coming down in large flakes—soft and puffy and already accumulating on top of the old snow.

I picked up my bike and struggled to roll it through the snow to the shed. I parked it by the old Harley. On the way back to the cabin, I noticed the ax leaning on the chopping block. I picked it up and saw the blood. I carried it inside with me and latched the door tight.

I planned for the long night ahead. First, I found the ancient kerosene lamp I'd noticed before, and I practiced lighting it. I'd need that once it got dark. There was a chair made from alder branches. I pulled it up by the fire and stationed myself there. My clothes eventually dried, and I put them back on. I was happy to get out of the hermit's stinky clothes.

I looked out the small window at the sky and realized this was going to be a major snowfall. My parents would be hysterical when I didn't return today. I knew it was futile, but I tried my cell again. No signal. No cellular miracle. As the light faded, I lit the lamp but soon realized I had limited fuel. I'd keep it on for a while, but after that I'd be alone in the dark. I located three small half-used candles. Not much for backup. I put more wood in the fire, but not too much. I was deathly afraid of a fire in the stovepipes. If that happened, this place would burn to the ground in minutes. I'd just keep it going with a low steady flame.

I checked Jonathan again. "Buddy," I said. "Yo, buddy?"

His eyes suddenly opened. "Where am I?" he muttered.

"You're home, Jonathan. You're right here."

"Is it safe?" he asked, whispering now, sounding scared.

"What do you mean?"

"Where's the enemy?" he asked in a quavering voice.

"There is no enemy," I said. "You're safe."

"Who are you?"

"Josh," I said. "Remember?"

"No," he said flatly. "How many did we kill?"

I wasn't prepared for that question. I said nothing. But it was starting to sink in.

"I'm wounded, aren't I?" he asked next.

"Yes. You need to stay in bed."

"But I'm safe, right?"

"You're safe. I'm here. I'm not going anywhere."

His eyes closed and he faded. I didn't know if he was dying or just falling asleep. The blankets rose and fell as he breathed, so all I could do was watch over him.

I began to imagine what had happened to Jonathan. He'd been outside splitting firewood with his ax when the helicopter flew over.

It frightened him, and he must have accidentally hit his leg with the blade and then crawled back into the house. It was a miracle he had not bled to death.

And it was a miracle that I had shown up.

But so far I was not of much use.

I stoked the fire again and studied the converted washing machine. The metal was rusted and thin in places. I didn't trust it. I kept inventory in my head of what I needed to do. Keep the fire going. Keep us warm. Keep Jonathan calm no matter how crazy he got. What if he had flashbacks of the war and tried to run out into the snow? He was in rough shape, and the effort could kill him. I'd never had so much responsibility in my life.

What if I had made the wrong decision? What if I should have gone for help? I pushed the thought out of my head and calmed myself down.

That's when I realized how hungry I was. Above me, hanging from the rafters, casting crazy shadows, were the dried eels. There were dozens of them—a full winter's supply. I stood up on the wobbly chair, tugged one down by the tail. I studied the puckered face of the snake-like creature. It was not exactly my idea of fine dining. I snapped off the head and bit into the flesh of the long body. The texture was like shoe leather, the taste was…well, it tasted like an eel that had been hanging from a rafter for a couple of months. I chewed and chewed, spit out some thin bones and swallowed.

At about nine o'clock, I turned off the lantern, checked on Jonathan and tucked matches and a candle in my pocket. I sat back in the chair and fell asleep. When I woke, the room was getting cool. I stoked the fire, and the place warmed quickly. I dozed again, woke, stoked the fire, catnapped. Outside, the snow was getting deeper and deeper. My parents would be frantic.

Jonathan woke in fright twice. Each time, he thought he was back in the war. Each time, I spoke to him patiently until he exhausted himself. The second time, just before fading again, he seemed to know where he was. "They'll want to take me away from here, won't they?" he asked.

"You need to get to a hospital," I said.

His eyes were wide-open, and I saw the fear again. "Please. Please, don't let them take me." And then his eyes shut.

I don't know what kept the old guy alive through the night. He'd lost a lot of blood, he'd nearly frozen to death before I found him, and he was out of his mind when he was awake. But he was alive.

As I sat in the dark, my mind grabbed on to all the things that could go wrong. The next time I checked on Jonathan, he could be dead, and I'd be here all alone with a dead man I had called a friend. If rescuers came by helicopter in the morning, the sound could trigger a flashback. And there was a good chance they would insist he be taken to a hospital. Jonathan would fight that with every inch of his life.

I was not great at my lonely post. Each time I woke, the cabin was cooling down. Twice I had to use the precious matches and birch bark to rekindle a flame in the stove. But eventually morning arrived. Jonathan had survived the night, but when I placed my hand on his forehead he felt hot. I wondered if his wound had an infection. Given his state of cleanliness, it seemed likely. This did not look good.

I put on the now-dry snowmobile suit and inched open the door. The snow had stopped, but it was chest high. As I opened the door further, soft powdery snow spilled into the room. I closed it quickly, worried we'd lose heat.

I decided the eel I ate for breakfast was my last. I'd search through Jonathan's supplies and learn to cook.

And then I heard the welcome buzz of snowmobiles in the distance. I closed my eyes. Yes. Definitely. Two of them far off but most certainly headed this way. My parents would have reported me missing. The rescue people would be out here along with everyone my dad knew who had a snowmobile. It was possible they would only look for me along the trail. They may not have a clue that I could be at the hermit's. Jonathan was snoring now. I had to take the chance. I had to get to the logging road.

I put a log in the fire, pulled on boots and zipped up the suit. I grabbed my gloves and plunged out into the snow-drift, hastily latching the door behind me. It was like swimming. The snow was chest high, and I kept sinking and having to climb out of drifts. I tried crawling along the surface of the soft snow. It coated my face, numbed my cheeks and gave me an ice-cream headache.

At the creek the snow was not quite so deep along the shoreline. As I stumbled out onto the logging road, I fell into the track where a snowmobile had already passed by. Darn.

But then I heard a second one headed my way and a third behind that. I yelled but soon realized they wouldn't hear me. I waited three long, panting minutes. A large black snowmobile approached and stopped. A blue one stopped right behind.

The driver of the first one popped off his helmet. It was Dave Jenkins. "Josh, you all right?"

I was still breathing so heavily, all I could do was nod.

"We got to get you home. You got frostbite?" He looked terribly concerned.

"No," I rasped. "It's Jonathan. He needs help. He cut himself badly. I stayed in his cabin last night."

He nodded. "Right. Hop on." I hopped on behind him and nodded to the driver behind him who followed.

Above the roar of the engine, he said, "That's Doctor Mahaney back there. He was one of the first to volunteer to come looking for you. He'll be right behind us." Dave revved the engine and plowed into the soft snow through the forest. He avoided getting stuck by ramming right through bushes and saplings. Without a helmet, the cascading snow blinded me and froze my face even more. I just hung on.

"We're almost there," Dave said.

Chapter Thirteen

When Doc Mahaney looked at Jonathan, he immediately said, "We have to get this man to a hospital."

He pulled out a two-way radio and was about to make the call when I grabbed it from him and said, "No. You can't do that."

He looked at me like I was crazy, but Dave shook his head and said,

"Josh is right. You call in a helicopter and this man is as good as dead."

"Then we rig up something to tow him out on a sled."

"If we move Jonathan," Dave said, "he'll lose it. He won't survive." Then turning to me he asked, "What was he like last night? Incoherent?"

"Sometimes. War stuff," I said.

He turned to Mahaney again. "There's no shrink in the world that can fix the damage in Jonathan. Living here keeps him alive."

Mahaney looked angry. He didn't get it. "You call that alive?"

It was a mean thing to say, but he had a point. Jonathan had remained unconscious and he was sweating. The doctor had removed my makeshift bandage. The gash looked dark and ugly.

"He's my friend," I said. "I'll stay here. Bring whatever you need here." I was staring at the old doctor.

Dave shrugged. "It's the only way. If he leaves here, he dies. If he stays and we can help him, I don't know. Maybe."

My dad was somewhere else on a snowmobile, helping to look for me. Dave got him on the radio. An hour later he showed up at the cabin. Mahaney had cleaned and bandaged the wound. More help was on the way. More medical supplies, food, a generator.

I rode home with my dad to talk to my mom, and then he and I both went back to Jonathan. We stayed the night. By the next day there were generators humming, tents set up, two nurses and Mahaney overseeing the operation. Jonathan seemed to enjoy the pampering.

It was amazing how generous people were. Some reporter got wind of the story, of course, and it was plastered in the newspaper and on TV. Everyone wanted to help. Jonathan was not going to take up any of the offers to move into a "better place" in town. He would stay put. But he had an army of new friends. As he got better, I saw a different side of Jonathan, a social side. He joked with Dave and the Doc.

My life was never quite the same after that. My parents had more respect for me. They bought me a satellite cell phone so I could call them from the most remote places on the planet. It had a GPS built in. I was like a tagged dolphin. If they wanted, they could know where I was at any time. I really didn't mind at all. In fact, it was kind of cool.

Everyone knew the story, so I became the center of attention for a while. Kids talked to me now. Sonia had a newfound interest in my well-being. She sent me emails and text messages all the time. Even Anton changed. Everyone stopped believing I had vandalized his bike.

I visited Jonathan often. My dad and I made snowmobile trips to see him until the snow thawed and my bike was back in action. Once the days started getting longer and the media lost interest in the hermit, I found myself riding down to Loggerman Creek and just sitting alone on a rock, feeling pretty good about things. Thinking that life as a hermit may not be all that bad.

Lesley Choyce divides his time between teaching, writing, running Pottersfield Press and hosting a television talk show. He is the author of over seventy books for youth and adults. *Reckless* is Lesley's third book in the Orca Currents series. Lesley lives in Lawrencetown Beach, Nova Scotia. For more information, visit www.lesleychoyce.com.

Titles in the Series

Orca currents